YOUR TOXIC TEETH

A GUIDE TO MERCURY POISONING FROM DENTAL FILLINGS

MURRAY J. VIMY, DMD

This book is written for educational purposes and is not intended to substitute for proper professional advice. The reader should seek appropriate consultation with their personal health care provider, prior to undertaking amalgam removal therapy.

ISBN: 0-9685926-0-0
Printed in Canada

Vimy, Murray J.
Your Toxic Teeth: mercury poisoning from dental fillings. Includes bibliographical references and index
1. Dental fillings
2. Mercury poisoning
3. Health

DEDICATION

To my little dark-haired girl - Bonnie

My love, I dedicate this book to you.
Our romance is the enduring lighthouse in my life.
You brighten my path and keep me steadfast.
For those times that I have ignored your needs in favour
of my mission, please forgive me.

TAKE THE
MERCURY SYMPTOM
QUESTIONAIRE

1. Subnormal Temperature   ____   ____
2. Chronic Fatigue   ____   ____
3. Muscle Spasms   ____   ____
4. Muscle Tremors   ____   ____
5. Jerky Gait   ____   ____
6. Numbness/Tingling   ____   ____
7. Joint Pains   ____   ____
8. Excessive perspiration esp at night   ____   ____
9. Uncontrolled blushing   ____   ____
10. Stomach Cramps   ____   ____
11. Persistent Cough   ____   ____
12. Chronic Sinusitis   ____   ____
13. Fluid accumulation   ____   ____
14. Restricted vision   ____   ____
15. Eyes sensitive to light   ____   ____
16. Difficulty seeing in the dark   ____   ____
17. Acne   ____   ____
18. Rashes/dry skin   ____   ____
19. Irreg. Blood Pressure   ____   ____
20. Swollen Glands   ____   ____
21. Bleeding Gums   ____   ____
22. Loose Teeth   ____   ____
23. Excessive salivation   ____   ____
24. Foul Breath   ____   ____
25. Metallic Taste   ____   ____
26. Sore Mouth   ____   ____
27. Mouth Ulcers   ____   ____
28. Burning Mouth   ____   ____
29. White Patches   ____   ____
30. Loss of Taste   ____   ____
31. Shortness of Breath   ____   ____
32. Irritability   ____   ____
33. Nervousness   ____   ____
34. Memory Loss   ____   ____

35. Shyness   ——   ——
36. Poor Concentration   ——   ——
37. Forgetfulness   ——   ——
38. Bursts of Anger   ——   ——
39. Depression   ——   ——
40. Anxiety   ——   ——
41. Insomnia   ——   ——
42. Apathy   ——   ——

This questionnaire is not to be used as a diagnostic test. However, the more symptoms you have, the greater the likelihood that you may have heavy metal poisoning. In particular, your exposure to mercury from dental "silver' fillings should be investigated.

CONTENTS

INTRODUCTION

"Ideally, then, a dental material that is to be used in the oral cavity should be harmless to the pulp and soft tissues. Also, it should contain no toxic diffusing substances that can be absorbed into the circulatory system to cause a systemic toxic response. The material should be free of potential sensitising agents that could lead to an allergic response, Finally, the material should have no carcinogenic potential."

Ralph Phillips (1982): <u>Skinner's Science of Dental Materials</u>, 8th ed. Philadelphia: W.B. Saunders Co, 311. Pp. 59 and 60.

This sounds good in theory but ...
If someone told you that you have large quantities of a known TOXIC substance implanted in your teeth and...

If someone told you that this implanted substance contained <u>mercury</u>, a heavy metal more dangerous than lead or arsenic; that it contained <u>copper</u>, a metal that is toxic to cells; and that it contained <u>silver</u>, a metal that disrupts your immune system...

If someone then told you that this implanted TOXIC substance was never properly tested for human safety and that your very OWN dentist placed it into <u>your</u> teeth...

If someone told you this, you would likely want a clear explanation

1

of all the facts, wouldn't you?

In December of 1990, the CBS NEWS 60 MINUTES program <u>Is there poison in your mouth?</u>, told of exactly these circumstances. Yet today, many people are still unaware of the seriousness of these facts!

The issue of mercury exposure from dental "silver" fillings has gained considerable notoriety in the general media during the last decade. Specific attention has focused on the potential for human health consequences and the general well being of the global environment. Hundreds of metric tonnes of mercury are placed into teeth world-wide each year and some of this material, as particulate waste from the dental office, finds its way into the sewerage and refuse systems, polluting our delicate environment.

Opposition from organised dentistry to the revelation has been swift. Claims by self-appointed dental "experts" that mercury/silver fillings are safe flies in the face of the growing body of medical experimental research evidence. Evidence published in respected peer-adjudicated medical research journals.

The scientific facts reviewed in this book are compelling. There is little scientific debate about the validity of these facts within the medical research community. However, the American and Canadian Dental Associations and their corporate dental manufacturing partners, under the direction of bureaucrats and dental academics, are waging a "media war" to sway public opinion. Their goal has been clearly expressed by the American Dental Association past-President - Dr. Geraldine Morrow:

> *"We are also working with our crisis management public relations firm to develop a strategy for reaching newspapers and other media throughout the country.... In addition to infection control, two issues the campaign is addressing are the safety of dental amalgam and the safety and effectiveness of fluoride ... Twelve consumer advisors and six topical experts have been selected and trained to serve as media spokespersons. In June we launched a nationwide media tour ..."* [1]

It would appear that organised dentistry is fixated in an outmoded

19th century paradigm, based on unscientific information. This mind set has resulted in the knee-jerk reaction, as exemplified by the statement made by Dr. Morrow.' Dentistry is in "future shock", hoping to quell a scientific debate with media propaganda.

Equally disconcerting is the presence of a group of health practitioners on the other extreme. They claim (also without scientific support) that mercury exposure from dental fillings is the cause of many serious medical problems for which the eitcology is not known. Moreover, they claim miraculous cures are possible with removal of the fillings.

The purpose of this book is to place the dental "silver" filling issue under the microscope of medical science and to give you, the reader, reliable information upon which to base decisions about YOUR TOXIC TEETH. Recommendations for the concerned patient regarding proper protocol for replacement of "silver" fillings with alternative safer dental materials will be discussed. It is hoped that this book will help to counteract the growing body of dental misinformation!

"SILVER" FILLINGS...
WHAT ARE THEY?

The term **"silver filling"** or **amalgam** purposefully misleads. A **"silver" filling**, contains 50% pure mercury, the same toxic mercury found in thermometers. Each **"silver" tooth filling** has approximately 750-1000 milligrams of this toxic mercury. Indeed, the term "amalgam", by definition, means "mixed with mercury"! Consequently, these tooth restorations should properly be called **mercury fillings**. Other metals included in the filling mixture are silver, copper, tin, and zinc.[1] So, every time your dentist refers to them as "silver" fillings or amalgam, an unspoken myth of safety is promulgated in a very deceptive way.

A mercury filling lasts about 7-9 years,[2,3] and when it fails the dentist usually replaces it with another mercury-containing filling. Thus, you unknowingly exchange a filling that is partially depleted of mercury for a new one loaded with fresh toxin. Approximately 75-80% of all tooth fillings are made from this mercury material[4]. Once covered with your saliva, the mercury filling begins to corrode, a rusting-like process. This corrosive breakdown becomes exaggerated if other dental treatments, containing other metals (e.g. gold), are also in the same mouth! The laws of physics and chemistry must be obeyed. It is impossible to have a stable mercury filling, one that does not breakdown. This explains why research has demonstrated that mercury containing dental fillings release mercury vapor and mercury-containing particles into your mouth continuously, all day long!

It is estimated that we take approximately 20,000 breaths in a day. Although each of these breaths only carries a minute quantity of mercury to your lungs and into your body, the cumulative effect of 20,000 breaths is clinically and toxicologically significant. In addition, the biochemical processes of the human body take approximately 70 days to rid just one day's mercury exposure. You see, your body acts like a dripping plugged sink. As long as the plug is in place, the sink fills, until it overflows. Thus, the mercury collects for years, until a sufficient quantity is in your tissues to produce adverse effects.

- **<u>CLINICAL RELEVANCE</u>**
  This time-release mercury exposure may be adversely affecting your health, slowly, on the installment plan, day by day, since even minute amounts of mercury can be very toxic.

ARE YOUR FILLINGS CERTIFIED SAFE?

The modern dental mercuy filling was introduced in 1812 by a British chemist. The "silvery paste", combined silver filings from coinage and liquid mercury and the material became fashionable for restoration of tooth cavities. Initially, problems occurred because the coins were not pure. This resulted in expansion of the "silvery" paste as it hardened in the cavity. Tooth-fractures and/or a "high bite" were often the result. From the outset, there was a concern within the dental profession regarding the issue of mercury-filling safety. This concern has resulted in cyclically recurring debates - called Amalgam Wars. Only recently has medical science rigorously tested the material for safety.

One such debate occurred in America during the mid-to late-1800s. The possibility of mercury toxicity from the "silver" fillings caused the American Society of Dental Surgeons to make mercury-filling usage an issue of malpractice. Member dentists had to sign an oath not to use mercury-containing materials in their practices. However, mercury-filling usage increased, because the material was very user friendly, because of its durability in the mouth, and because it allowed the dentist to deliver less expensive care (thus affording him a competitive economic advantage). This economic advantage caused many dentists to refuse the oath and membership in the professional society. By 1856, the American Society of Dental

Surgeons was forced to disband due to dwindling membership. In its place arose the American Dental Association founded by those who advocated and used mercury-fillings.[1-3] Again in the 1920s, a controversy erupted. A German chemistry professor published research articles and scientific letters attacking mercury-filling usage on the basis of possible mercury toxic effects.[4-9] The dental profession's opinion prevailed and the controversy abated, even though there was no significant scientific evidence to support the claim of mercury-filling safety.

Today, almost two centuries after the introduction of the "modern" mercury filling and still without a shred of scientific evidence to support its recommendations, the American Dental Association has amended its Code of Ethics to make the removal of serviceable mercury-fillings an issue of <u>unethical</u> conduct. Presently, it is viewed as unethical to replace mercury fillings if the reason for filling removal is to:

1. Eliminate a toxic material from the human body or
2. When this recommendation is made solely by the dentist.[10,11]

In the American Dental Association's view, a dentist is "ethical" to place the mercury material and recommend its safety. But, if the dentist suggests that the mercury fillings are potentially harmful or that exposure to unnecessary toxic mercury can result, then the dentist is acting "unethically". Yet in the same breath, the American Dental Association considers it ethical conduct to remove clinically serviceable mercury fillings if done for aesthetic reasons (to make the smile pretty), if done at the request of a physician, or if done at the patient's request (without prompting by the dentist).

Both the general public and dentists believe that the mercury tooth filling material is certified "safe for human use" by the American and Canadian Dental Associations (ADA, CDA), the United States Food and Drug Administration (USFDA) and Health Canada. Although the A.D.A. and C.D.A. recommend mercury fillings for the majority of tooth cavities and promote the notion of safety, **they do not <u>certify</u> them as safe!**[12] The ADA <u>only</u> certifies the purity of the metal components, separately. They do not certify the filling mixture made by the dentist and placed into your teeth! This is a shocking revelation to some. But in fact, the Dental Associations do not have the legal authority to certify dental materials. So, the American Dental Association certifies the mercury put in to the filling mixture as 99.999% pure - pure poison that is!

In North America, only governmental regulatory agencies such as the United States Food and Drug Administration (USFDA) and Health Canada have the authority to regulate medical products and devices. But, again, the USFDA only certifies the purity of the metal components, separately. They do not certify the filling mixture made by the dentist and placed into your teeth.[13] The USFDA certifies the mercury put into the filling mixture made by your dentist as 99.999% pure - pure poison that is!

Therefore, your fillings are neither certified nor approved by the dental profession or the government! What assurance do you have that this tooth filling material is safe for you and your family? **Absolutely none!**

Even more amazing is the occupational recommendations by both the A.D.A. and C.D.A. Councils on Dental Materials and Equipment instructing dental personnel to follow a strict protocol when handling mercury, mercury filling material and other mercury-containing materials.[14] A no-touch technique must be followed to protect the dentist and the dental personnel from the toxic effects of mercury!

Moreover, the U.S. Environmental Protection Agency (USEPA) defines scrap mercury filling material as a biohazard waste. A toxic biohazard that, by law, must be sealed in leak-proof, fluid-filled containers and carted out of the dental office by licensed hazard control experts in armoured trucks. Yet at the same time, the dental profession considers this material to be absolutely safe, once it is implanted permanently into your body - into your teeth.[11, 12]

The paradoxical question is...

DENTAL OPINION
Versus SCIENCE

DENTAL OPINION #1:
Once the mercury is mixed with the other metals, it is locked into the filling and cannot come out.[1]

THE SCIENTIFIC FACTS:
Mercury vapor is released continuously from dental fillings. This vapor release is enhanced by chewing [2,3], tooth brushing [4] and eating thermally hot, salty and acidic foods.[5] The more mercury fillings you have and/or the larger the chewing surface area, the larger will be your daily exposure to mercury.[2] Once chewing stops, it takes approximately 90 minutes until the rate of mercury release declines back to the lower pre-chewing level.[3]

- ### CLINICAL RELEVANCE
  You are on a roller coaster of mercury vapor exposure during the day. Breakfast will cause the mercury release to increase and just as the release slows, it is time for the midmorning coffee break. Up goes your exposure again! This pattern repeats for lunch, mid-afternoon coffee, dinner, and a snack before bedtime. If you chronically chew gum or grind your teeth, you are exposed to even very high levels of mercury, continuously!

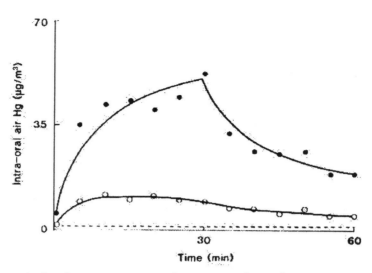

Figure 1 is from a research paper that demonstrates this phenomenon. Human subjects were divided into 3 groups, a group with 12 or more biting surface mercury fillings (•), a group with 4 or fewer biting surface mercury fillings (o) and a control group (---) with no fillings. Before testing the concentration of mercury in the mouth air, the subjects were instructed not to eat, drink, chew anything, or bush their teeth for 1 hour. At time zero, an intra-oral mercury measurement was made. Then each subject was given sugarless gum to chew for 5 minutes. At 5 minutes, the gum was spit out and a new measure was taken. Fresh gum was then given and this procedure was repeated for six times. At 30 minutes, all gum chewing stopped, but mercury measures were taken for six additional 5-minute periods. Each of these up-down cycles, as seen in the graph, is equivalent to one meal or snack.

DENTAL OPINION #2:
"... published studies have demonstrated the release of mercury vapor into the mouth after gum chewing. But this is not necessarily an exposure (get into body tissues). Exhaled air is not inhaled air," says Dr. Sheldon Newman, Dental Professor formerly at the University of Alberta and now at the University of Colorado (1984, Ontario Dentist).

THE SCIENTIFIC FACTS:
German[6] Swedish and American autopsy investigations[7,8] found that

human brain and kidney tissues from individuals who had mercury fillings contained significantly higher mercury levels than tissue samples from individuals who had no mercury fillings! Furthermore, the concentration of brain mercury in the subjects with dental mercury fillings correlated with the number of mercury fillings present. That is, the more fillings one had in one's mouth, the greater the brain tissue mercury level. It has been demonstrated experimentally that mercury specifically released from tooth fillings is readily absorbed into body tissues.[9]

Most significantly, prospective animal studies demonstrate that mercury coming from dental fillings can be found in all tissues, after only 30 days of chewing.

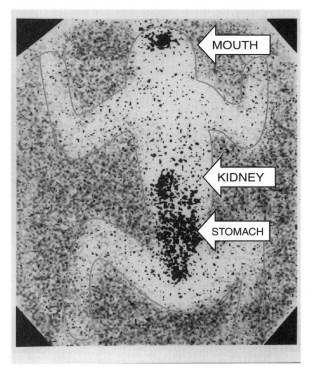

Figure 2 is a whole body image scan of a monkey who had 12 biting-surface mercury fillings placed in his teeth. He chewed food with them, normally, for 30 days. These fillings are identical to the mercury fillings placed in your mouth by your dentist, except that 10% of the mercury had a radioactive tag. Radioactive mercury does

12

not occur naturally. It must be made radioactive in a nuclear reactor. Thus, any tagged mercury that showed up in the monkey's tissues had to come from the fillings! When tested in a radioactive counter, all monkey tissues had some radioactive mercury. Some tissues were so laden with radioactivity that it shows up as dark areas in the whole-body image scan. You can clearly see the dark areas in the mouth, the stomach/intestines and the left and right kidneys.

- **CLINICAL RELEVANCE**
  It is now scientifically established that your dental mercury fillings constitute your largest single source of inorganic mercury exposure, <u>larger than all other environmental sources combined</u> including air, water and food[10] The average daily absorbed dose from fillings is approximately 12 micrograms.[11]

Despite these replicated scientific findings, the American and Canadian Dental Associations maintain that mercury fillings are totally safe.[12] Incredibly, they base this <u>opinion</u> on the following anecdotal facts: "silver" fillings have been used for 150 years; billions of fillings have been placed; and dentists do not see anyone sick or dying from the mercury exposure. Death is not the issue, but poor health is. Moreover, dentists are neither trained nor licensed to make medical diagnoses about an individual's general health status.[13] Yet from the medical perspective, mercury fillings are considered your most significant mercury source, having serious potential for toxic impact on your health. So, while the dental profession obfuscates, medical researchers continue investigating the possible health implications of dental mercury exposure.

Although clinical reports suggest a relationship between dental mercury fillings and human health, it is only recently that research has established a direct cause and effect link between mercury fillings and pathology.

BODY TISSUES AT GREATEST RISK

1. THE KIDNEY
The latest medical research demonstrates that mercury from "silver" fillings accumulates in all adult tissues, being highest in the kidney and liver.[14] Experimental animal evidence clearly shows that kidney

function can be reduced after dental filling placement.[15] This is very significant, since your kidneys remove harmful substances from the blood, maintain blood pressure, your body's level of hydration, and reabsorbs needed nutrients and minerals. Especially at risk to mercury filling placement are those who already have kidney disease or whose family have a genetic predisposition to kidney disease.

- **CLINICAL RELEVANCE**
  Based on this medical evidence, it would seem prudent that mercury fillings should not be placed in individuals who have kidney disease or a family history of such problems.

2. BRAIN & NERVE TISSUE

Within the brain and associated tissues, the mercury level is highest in the pituitary gland, the master gland of the body. Scientific reports now implicate inorganic mercury in the biochemical pathology of certain brain and nervous system disorders. Human autopsy data has demonstrated significantly higher mercury concentrations in Alzheimer's brains than in age-matched control brains not having Alzheimer's Disease. The mercury was particularly high in brain areas associated with memory. The authors suggest that dental amalgam is the most likely source of the mercury.[16,17] Another research group has isolated the biochemical pathway that when blocked by mercury[18] results in brain nerve tangles characteristic of Alzheimer's pathology.[19] Furthermore, recent research has suggested the possible relationship between dental mercury fillings and Alzheimer's Disease.[20] Mercury poisoning may also mimic Multiple Sclerosis and Parkinson's Disease.

- **CLINICAL RELEVANCE**
  Based on the medical evidence, individuals having neurological disorders or diseases such as Alzheimer's, Parkinson's Disease, Multiple Sclerosis or A.L.S. or a family history of such diseases, are well advised to avoid mercury fillings. Certain psychological and psychiatric disorders can also be induced or exacerbated by mercury exposure.

3. THE UNBORN & NEWBORN

Dental mercury will also cross the placenta and accumulate in the developing unborn baby within two days after the fillings are placed in the mother's teeth.[14]   Mother's milk has also been shown to contain mercury from the fillings, suggesting that the new-born would have an additional exposure.[21]

- **CLINICAL RELEVANCE**
  Based on the medical evidence, dental treatment involving the placement or removal of mercury fillings must be avoided during pregnancy and during the period of breast-feeding. Chronic mercury exposure may also affect one's ability to get pregnant.

4. THE STOMACH AND INTESTINES

Normal bacteria in the intestines help us digest food and make vitamins available for absorption. These friendly bacteria are killed or altered by exposure to mercury from the "silver" fillings. In their place, strains of mercury-resistant bacteria appear.[15]   This effect is a very significant medical finding, because bacteria that are mercury resistant are also antibiotic resistant. Thus, exposure to mercury from dental fillings might be one reason to explain the growing ineffectiveness of antibiotics, today.

- **CLINICAL RELEVANCE**
  Based on the medical evidence, individuals with digestive and bowel disorders should consider avoiding unwarranted mercury exposure from dental fillings.

Based on the overwhelming scientific evidence WE KNOW THE FOLLOWING...

In general

1. Mercury is an extremely dangerous poison.

2. There is no safe level of mercury exposure for humans.

3. Dental "silver" fillings contain 50% pure elemental mercury.

In specific

1. Mercury is released continuously from mercury fillings, because these fillings are chemically <u>un</u>stable.

2. In humans, mercury fillings produce a pharmacologically

significant daily dose of poisonous mercury.

3. Mercury fillings are the largest source of toxic mercury exposure in the general population.

4. Toxic mercury released from mercury fillings collects in <u>all</u> adult human tissues, being highest in the kidney, liver and then the brain.

5. Dental mercury crosses the placenta and collects in the developing unborn baby and exposes the new born via mother's milk.

6. Mercury from dental fillings reduces kidney function.

7. Mercury from dental fillings alters the normal bacterial populations in the intestinal tract, producing antibiotic resistance.

8. Mercury from dental fillings has been implicated in nervous system disorders such as Alzheimer's Disease.

The issue of mercury filling safety is no longer a medical scientific debate. Today, the medical scientific evidence overwhelmingly disproves the <u>unsupported opinion</u> of the dental profession! For further historical discussion of this issue the reader is referred to a comprehensive medical review article.[22]

SYMPTOMS OF MERCURY POISONING

Mercury can cause a variety of seemingly unrelated symptoms.[1-3] Many of these symptoms are nonspecific and therefore could easily be misdiagnosed as having resulted from other environmental contaminants or medical conditions. Indeed, mercury exposure has been called the "great masquerader".[4]

The similarity of mercury related symptoms to other medical conditions make it very difficult for physicians to arrive at the correct diagnosis. Moreover, only recently has the medical profession become aware of the mercury exposure from dental tooth fillings. Most dentists are of little help with the diagnosis of mercury poisoning, because they lack the appropriate medical training and because they assume that once the dental filling is mixed the mercury is locked in and "it's toxic properties are made harmless".

SYMPTOMS OF MERCURY POISONING

1. Psychological disturbances

Irritability	Nervousness
Shyness or timidity	Loss of memory
Lack of attention	Low self-confidence
Decline in intellect	Lack of self-control
Fits of anger	Depression
Anxiety	Drowsiness or Insomnia

2. Mouth symptoms

Bleeding gums	Loose teeth
Bone loss around teeth	Excessive saliva
Metallic taste	Foul breath
Stomatitis	White patches

- Ulcerations
- Burning mouth
- Tissue pigmentations.

3. General health effects

a.) Gastrointestinal effects

Regular abdominal cramps
Chronic constipation or diarrhoea
Chronic gastritis

b.) Cardiovascular (heart)

Irregular heart rates (slow or fast)
Feeble or irregular pulse
Alterations in blood pressure
Pain and/or pressure in the chest

c.) Neurological

Fine tremors (hands, feet, lips, eyelids)
Chronic headaches
Dizziness
Ringing in the ears

d.) Respiratory

Persistent cough
Emphysema
Shallow or irregular respiration

e.) Immunological
Allergies
Asthma
Rhinitis
Sinusitis
Swollen lymph nodes (especially in the neck)
Autoimmunity

f.) Endocrine
Subnormal body temperature
Cold clammy skin (especially hands and feet)
Excessive perspiration

g.) Skin
Sores on the skin face, and shoulders

h.) Kidney
Electrolyte imbalance (minerals)
Reduction in kidney filtering
Renal Failure in severe cases
Glomerular nephritis

4. Other
Muscle weakness
Joint pain
Chronic Fatigue
Anaemia
Loss of appetite
Weight loss
Constriction of the visual field

A note of caution is appropriate at this point in the discussion. As you can see from the foregoing list, just about any health problem would appear as if it is caused by mercury from dental fillings. **This of course is faulty logic!**

Mercury exposure has not been identified as the sole cause of any specific medical illnesses, except for one - MERCURY POISONING. In addition, science has not determined a level, at which, one is safe from the toxic and allergic effects of mercury. Although your body has biochemical methods to detoxify you, the strength of this system varies from person-to-person. Each of us is biochemically different, to some extent unique. Consequently, some individuals have specific biochemical weaknesses, making them more susceptible, even to low daily doses of mercury.

The decision to remove one's fillings must be done with complete understanding of this fact. Nevertheless, filling removal does produce benefits in some people, because it removes a chronic source of a very toxic heavy metal, freeing up one's biochemistry and immune system to deal with what nature intended.

MERCURY FILLINGS
AND DISEASES

POISONING
Mercury vapor is odorless, colorless, tasteless, and can easily cross the lung into the blood. Once in the bloodstream the mercury vapor enters the cells where it is activated. In this active state, it attaches itself to sulfur containing enzymes.[1]

Enzymes, specialized chemical molecules in the cell, make chemical reactions occur by bringing together other molecules so that they can react with each other. Without enzymes, there would not be life as we know it, since the random collision of molecules would not be sufficiently frequent or ordered to produce metabolism and energy. Mercury's primary mode of action is as an enzyme poison and the net effect is metabolic sickness.[1]

ALLERGY
One can also be allergic to mercury and to the other metal components in the filling mixture. These allergic reactions can be systemic or local, occurring either immediately at the initial exposure or after a delay of many years.[2-5] The symptoms can include:[6]

a. Eczema and sores on the face and shoulders
b. Burning and dry mouth, swelling of the lips, tongue and mucosa, and malaise or fever

Less dramatic effects may also occur. But, these have not been thoroughly investigated.

- **CLINICAL RELEVANCE**
  If you are allergic to jewelry (ie. swollen ears to ear rings or your wrists turns black from your watch), how are you reacting to your mouth jewelry - your dental fillings?

DENTAL OPINION #3:

Mercury exposure from "silver" fillings is of no medical concern except for those few individuals mercury allergic, believed to be much less than 1% of the total population.[7]

THE SCIENTIFIC FACTS:

This less than 1% hypothesis is patently false. Medical scientific research evidence clearly shows that the incidence of mercury allergy in the general North American population is approximately 5%.[8] Thus, 5 of every 100 patients in a dental practice are allergic to the fillings in their mouths.

- **CLINICAL RELEVANCE:**
  On this basis alone, the mercury tooth filling material should be removed from the market by the government regulators.

MERCURY CAN INDUCE AUTOIMMUNITY

Mercury induces an immunological reaction, which in medicine is called autoimmunity.[9,10] Here the body's immune system, which is designed to protect "you" from infections and cancer cell formation ("not-you"), loses it's ability to differentiate between the healthy cells in your body and the diseased cells that must be removed. Thus, the immune system confuses "you" for "not-you" and proceeds to destroy your otherwise healthy tissue. There are many specific autoimmune diseases; for example, Multiple Sclerosis, Lupus, Autoimmune Glomerular Nephritis (a kidney disease) etc. Presently, there is **insufficient experimental evidence** to conclude that mercury fillings are the sole cause of these problems.

If you are told that removal of mercury fillings will <u>cure</u> you, be extremely cautious. Filling removal is not a magic bullet. Removing the source of chronic mercury exposure is a positive health choice, because it eliminates a toxic heavy metal burden from your body's chemistry. It is not a proven cure for any specific disease - other than mercury poisoning!

IDIOSYNCRATIC REACTIONS

Although individuals may be hypersensitive (allergic) or sensitive (toxic) to low level mercury exposure, some individuals have atypical idiosyncratic (unusual) reactions to chemicals such as mercury.[12,13] Due to an individual's genetic make up and/or exposure to other environmental contaminants, they may be even more sensitive to low levels of mercury. Often their symptoms are bizarre and do not fit the typical mercury exposure pattern. Individuals that respond in this manner are called "environmentally sensitive" persons. They are not medically or biochemically average. They are unique and difficult to diagnose and treat (see Appendix 1).

Whether or not dental fillings cause specific diseases is an important issue facing medical research today. There are many "diseases" whose causes have not as yet been identified. However to date, evidence that specific diseases are directly the sole result of exposure to mercury fillings is tentative at best. **Still, mercury exposure from any source and in any amount will cause mercury poisoning.** Therefore, one should not ignore mercury dental fillings, as an important negative factor on one's general health. Mercury, more toxic than lead or arsenic, can cause cell death or irreversible chemical damage to cells well before visible symptoms occur.

There are many individual cases of clinical improvements to certain medical conditions after mercury filling removal and replacement (CBS NEWS 60 MINUTES, December 16, 1990). Some dental professionals view these "cures" as merely placebo effects or cases of spontaneous recoveries. Others suggest that there is a pattern deserving continuing serious medical investigation.

- **CLINICAL RELEVANCE**
  All exposures to mercury should be avoided, especially from dental fillings. It is also prudent for some individuals to remove their mercury fillings and replace them with more compatible, safe materials. This is suggested not to produce a "cure", but rather as a positive health-choice that eliminates a significant continuous daily source of toxic mercury exposure.

23

YOUR
MERCURY EXPOSURE

Determining the impact of chronic low-dose mercury exposure on human health has proved to be very difficult. No one-laboratory test is 100% accurate, but laboratory investigations can help to:

1. Evaluate overall health status and identify other medical factors.
2. Identify lifestyle factors, such as diet, which may need modification.
3. Determine the need for therapeutic intervention.
4. Monitor organ performance (e.g. kidney and liver function)
5. Monitor recovery by tracking mercury excretion from the body.

INTRA-ORAL VAPOUR TEST
Developed at the University of Calgary Medical Faculty, this is by far the most useful and cost effective test of exposure to mercury from dental fillings. This test is well documented in the scientific literature[1-4] and will aid in determining the extent of mercury being released from dental fillings daily, under controlled chewing conditions. With this information, one can estimate one's potential tissue mercury levels.[5]

BLOOD AND URINE MERCURY LEVELS
It is well known that the level of mercury found in blood, urine and hair may not necessarily correlate with clinical symptoms of

mercury poisoning. Both low and high urinary mercury level may indicate a problem. The high urinary level suggests the possibility of a recent large exposure or alternatively the tissue release of stored mercury. On the other hand, low urinary mercury might indicate little exposure or could reflect that the mercury is in the tissue and is unavailable for urinary excretion. So, a series of blood and/or urine mercury tests before and after treatment could aid in assessing whether detoxification (elimination from the body) of the mercury is proceeding successfully.

DMPS CHALLENGE TEST
This new test involves urine mercury analysis before and after a challenge with a chelation drug that helps the body to liberate stored mercury. This test is more accurate than the straightforward blood or urine test described above.[6]

FAECAL MERCURY LEVEL
Although seldom done, this is the most accurate method of assessing the extent of mercury exposure, since the largest portion of mercury is excreted via the intestinal route in bile. However, finding a laboratory that does this test may prove to be difficult.

HAIR MINERAL ANALYSIS
Hair analysis is of little value.

SKIN PATCH TESTING - HYPERSENSITIVITY
The patch test is controversial.[7] Some clinicians suggest that the patch test could worsen the symptoms; while other do not hold that view. There is also not full agreement on what constitutes a proper test and what reactions indicate a positive response. Moreover, individuals who are pregnant, or who suffer severe medical conditions should not take the mercury patch test. A trained professional such as a medical dermatologist or allergist is appropriate to administer the patch testing. It should be done with ammoniated mercury, not mercury chloride, because mercury chloride produces false positive results.

SYMPTOM PROFILE
A helpful method to assess the possibility of mercury exposure is to determine your symptom profile by completing a comprehensive

medical history. Since mercury poisoning can mimic a whole array of conditions and since most of the symptoms relating to low dose exposure are non-specific, a symptom survey is only useful when taken into consideration with other more objective measures of mercury measurement (See Chapter 4 and the Mercury Symptom Questionaire on Page V)

OTHER EXPERIMENTAL TESTS
a. Immune cell function
b. Presence of mercury-resistant bacteria
c. Galvanic (electrical) testing
d. Organ function tests (e.g. kidney filtration rate)

As you can readily see, determining the role and effects of mercury under low-dose continuous exposure conditions is difficult and costly. At present, the Intra-oral Vapor Test and the DMPS Challenge Test are the least expensive and most useful methods of determining relative exposure to mercury from the dental fillings.

If you have a serious medical problem that you feel may be related to mercury exposure, it is essential that you keep your physician fully informed of your concerns and proposed dental therapy.

WHEN TO REMOVE YOUR MERCURY FILLINGS?
The following represents the reasonable criteria for mercury-filling removal based upon published scientific data and clinical experience. Mercury fillings can be removed if:

1. It is your request to have this toxic material removed and replaced. After all, it is your body and you have the right to choose the materials you want placed in it.

2. In the opinion of your attending physician mercury filling removal will aid your general health or if the mercury exposure is a contributing factor to your medical condition.

3. You have a positive mercury patch test, indicating hypersensitivity to mercury. Five percent (5%) of North Americans are mercury allergic.

4. In the dentist's opinion, pre-existing mercury filling has ceased to be serviceable (e.g. The filling is cracked, broken or has decay).

5. In the dentist's opinion, the presence of the mercury fillings is producing harmful oral pathology, such as, burning mouth, mouth sores, gum disease and pre-cancerous white patches in the mouth.

6. You fail an Intra-oral Mercury Vapor Test or DMPS Challenge, finding an excessive level of mercury exposure. The dentist or physician can then make the recommendation to have the mercury fillings replaced to eliminate a chronic environmental source of exposure to a toxic heavy metal (mercury), irrespective of whether you are sick or in good health.

ALTERNATIVES TO MERCURY

Dental mercury fillings have been the treatment of choice for dental decay for almost 200 years. The main reasons for its popularity are ease of use, durability and low cost. However, the mercury material is not biocompatible, because of the metal content, especially the mercury. The mercury filling material has many physical advantages. But, its disadvantage of bio<u>in</u>compatibility, makes it contraindicated for human use. An <u>ideal</u> dental restorative material does not yet exist. After all, nothing is as good as the original tooth. But, satisfactory alternatives to mercury fillings are available.[1,2]

Dentistry, unlike medicine, offers levels of care from the barely adequate to excellent. Contrary to popular belief, some dentists specialize in the barely adequate, while others are committed to excellence. However, everyone deserves to have a proper diagnosis and treatment plan. Everyone has the right to be fully informed. Most people can afford proper quality dental care. It is merely a matter of good planning.

- **<u>CLINICAL RELEVANCE</u>**
  If it is determined you might benefit from mercury removal, then replace your mercury fillings at a rate your time and budget will allow.

ALTERNATIVE MATERIALS

• THE METALS
I. GOLD ALLOY RESTORATIONS
a. Direct Gold Foil

Two types of gold materials are employed in dentistry. First is gold foil. This consists of small foiled pellets of pure gold, like aluminum foil only thinner. Pure gold has the unique property of being able to chemically bond to itself, even at room temperature. Thus, the filling is made by adding the pure gold in increments into the prepared cavity and "pounding" each pellet onto the next.

Gold foil has some serious <u>disadvantages.</u>

1. The procedure is very time consuming and expensive.

2. Since pure gold is very soft, gold foil can only be used in non-chewing areas.

3. It is not very attractive, especially on front teeth.

4. The "pounding" procedure can itself be very traumatic, sometimes causing tooth fractures and abscesses.

b. Gold castings (indirect)

Gold castings, such as inlays, onlays and crowns (caps), are the most widely used gold tooth restorations. These restorations are not pure gold, but gold alloyed with other metals to increase the strength of the restoration. These are made in a laboratory, like jewelry, on a mold made from your teeth.

The <u>advantages</u> of cast gold restorations are:

1. The harder gold alloy can be used in biting surface tooth restorations.

2. Gold casting restorations do not corrode readily and maintain their shine. Consequently, bacteria and food do not easily stick to the gold restoration.

3. Gold castings fit very accurately.

4. Gold casting restorations are fabricated in the laboratory where time can be taken to develop a proper "bite", establish proper contours to deflect food from the gums, and to ensure tight contact between adjacent teeth so food does not impact between the teeth. This helps to control gum disease.

5. The tooth preparation is conservative and less tooth needs to be removed.

Disadvantages of gold casting restorations are:

1. The dentist must be very skilled; preparing and fitting cast restorations is very demanding.

2. The cast restoration is held in place by a dental adhesive, which does not strengthen the tooth as bonding does (bonding discussed below for porcelain and ceramic-resin).

3. Some individuals do not like the appearance of gold, even on molar and bicuspid teeth.

4. Some individuals may be sensitive to the metallic components of the gold alloy.

Still, gold alloy cast restorations are excellent tooth restorations.

II. NON-PRECIOUS METAL ALLOYS

During the mid to late 1970s when the price of gold skyrocketed, other alloys containing little or no gold were introduced into dentistry. These alloys, containing high levels of base metals, have been shown to corrode readily, release metallic components into the saliva, and may be potentially harmful to some individuals. If you decide to have metallic restorations insist on high quality gold/platinum alloys, the more gold and platinum the better. For example, many people are allergic to nickel. Today, nickel-containing restorations are widely used. If your body reacts to costume jewelry, if your hand breaks into a rash or turns black around your ring or watch, then be careful what you select for your "mouth jewelry".

Do not sacrifice safety to save a few dollars! It may prove costly to your health in the end.

III. TITANIUM METAL ALLOY

Recently, titanium metal has been employed in dental restorations. Titanium is very biocompatible and has been used in medicine for hip and other joint replacements. This material may help answer the problem of biocompatibility. Moreover, titanium is extremely durable, strong and relatively non-reactive electrochemically. It is an alternative that you should consider with your dentist!

• PORCELAIN

Dental porcelains consist of crystalline minerals, such as feldspar, silica, and alumina, in a glass matrix. The finely ground glass particles fuse together at high temperature to form a translucent enamel-like material.

The <u>advantages</u> of porcelain restorations are:

1. Natural tooth-like appearance.

2. They are very durable when properly glazed and do not collect dental plaque readily.

The <u>disadvantages</u> are:

1. Brittleness (subject to breakage under stress).

2. Abrasiveness (tend to wear the opposing natural tooth prematurely).

3. Difficulty obtaining an accurate fit.

Recent techniques of bonding porcelain to the tooth have helped to overcome the fitting problem. This bonding process dramatically increases the strength of the porcelain restoration and may also impart additional strength to the tooth itself. Porcelain restorations can also be cemented into place with dental adhesive cement, but this procedure does not improve the performance of the restoration.

• CERAMIC-RESIN RESTORATIONS

The resin materials were developed primarily because of their aesthetic properties. However, today the concern for biocompatibility predominates. If used properly, resins are one of the best replacements for mercury fillings. The composite resin, which consists of a microscopic glass particle filled Bis-GMA resin, is widely used today. These materials have been employed in front teeth in non-chewing areas for many years. Their success has been outstanding and has improved significantly with the new bonding procedures. The original resins did not have a lot of glass particle filler and were not suitable for grinding surfaces because they abraded easily. By developing techniques to add more and more glass particles to the material, the wear resistance has been improved to the point that under certain circumstances the composite resin materials can be used in molar and bicuspid grinding teeth. The composite resin materials can be placed either directly in the tooth or they can be processed in the laboratory as inlays or onlays and then bonded into the tooth.

a. Ceramic-resin <u>direct</u> (composites)

Using ceramic resin directly in the tooth means that the tooth is drilled and filled at the same appointment. The composite resin material is added in increments to the cavity and cured with a high intensity daylight gun. This process is widely known as bonding. Such direct application of composite resin is limited. Only small biting surface fillings can be restored successfully with this technique. Although many dentists believe that larger fillings are also successful, the track record is very mixed. At the recent time, the technology of direct composite resin is best used for small fillings.

If used appropriately the <u>advantages</u> of direct composite are:

1. Biocompatibility (no mercury),

2. Durability.

3. Aesthetics

4. Reduced electrical current (little corrosion).

5. Enhancement of tooth strength due to bonding process.

6. Cost effectiveness.

There are, however, <u>disadvantages:</u>

1. The light curing in the mouth only polymerizes approximately 70% of the resin, thus, 30% of the resin material does not react. This means that the partially set material is not as strong or wear-resistant as it could be. Hence, this technique should only be employed in small restorations as described previously.

2. Some individuals can respond adversely to exposure to the non-reacted resin. This reaction often takes the form of an allergy, especially for those who are petroleum sensitive. But, generally, the material appears to be compatible and it does not contain poisonous metals, such as mercury.

3. The incremental process of directly bonding ceramic/resin produces shrinkage or contraction of the composite material. If not done properly, this can result in open margins and leakage, producing tooth sensitivity and recurrent areas of decay around the filling. Thus, this type of filling may not last as long as one might hope.

4. Tooth sensitivity can also result from the mild acid used during the bonding procedure especially in deep restorations.

5. Composite resin restorations are very demanding of the dentist's skills.

b. Ceramic-resin <u>indirect</u> laboratory processed inlays
A method to overcome many of the drawbacks of the direct resin bonded filling is to use the same material, but process it in the laboratory, under heat and pressure.

Advantages of laboratory resin restorations are:

1. Laboratory processing ensures that shrinkage can be controlled.

2. Most of the resin is chemically reacted. The material is more durable. Shrinkage occurs before placement in the tooth and thus sensitivity is eliminated.

3. There are no open margins between the tooth and the restoration because shrinkage is limited to the thin bonding layer.

4. The final restoration is made in the laboratory and all the advantages discussed under gold alloy restorations are also realized.

5. The result is an aesthetically pleasing, durable, cost-effective tooth restoration.

6. These restorations have the same advantages as the bonded porcelain restorations discussed previously.

7. Larger more complex restorations are possible, since processing under heat and pressure enhances the materials strength and abrasive resistant qualities.

8. A laboratory processed composite restoration will wear at almost the same rate as tooth enamel, making it also physically compatible in the mouth.

Disadvantages of laboratory resin restorations are:

1. Composite resin restorations are very demanding of the dentist's skills.

• GLASS IONOMER TREATMENTS

Some individuals cannot afford total care immediately. In these cases, the following is suggested. First, if it has been established that there are reasonable medical or dental criteria (indicating your mercury fillings may be contributing to your problems), the following are satisfactory interim treatments.

1. Replace small mercury fillings with glass ionomer base fillings. These are not very durable but they should allow you to rid yourself of the mercury and give you 6-18 months to slowly replace the glass ionomer with other materials.

2. Your goal should be to rehabilitate one side of your mouth as soon as your budget allows with quality dentistry. Then, you will be able to eat comfortably with a strong non-mercury mouth. Take the crisis out of the situation.

If your general health is not a problem but economics is and you want to remove the mercury from your mouth because it is a positive health choice, then follow recommendation #2 above. Rehabilitate your mouth as your time and budget allow. Plan for it, and follow through.

MIXING METALS IN THE MOUTH

It is important that different metals not be in close proximity in the mouth. In fact, even if they are far apart serious problems can occur. First, dissimilar metals form an electrical link to each other by the saliva. For example gold will attract electrons from the components of mercury fillings, causing corrosion (rusting). This corrosive process releases more mercury than would normally be the case. Second, the electrical currents produced can have serious effects on mouth tissue such as blistering, burning mouth and bleeding gums.

PHILOSOPHY OF METAL FREE DENTISTRY

The solutions in this book go far beyond the mercury issue. Metal in the human body is usually not tolerated well. Tomorrow's dentist may very well practice metal free not just mercury-free dentistry. However, you cannot judge yesterday's dentistry by today's standards. The standards are changing rapidly as new scientific research is published. Other metal dental appliances, such as, chrome/cobalt partial dentures should also be avoided, especially by the metal sensitive individual. Thermoplastic replacements are now available. Some are not as durable as the metal, but they do not produce electrochemical corrosion, or metal ions to which many individuals react.

WHAT MATERIAL IS BEST FOR YOU?

The need to assess the suitability, safety and biocompatibility of restorative materials prior to placement has been widely recognized. The ability to measure the presence of a toxic material is often difficult, and even if detected, the amount of the toxic material needed to provoke an adverse reaction varies from individual to individual. When the human body encounters a toxic or noxious substance, the immune system generally produces a defense against it by making specific antibodies to the offending material. The presence of these antibodies can be tested and used as an indicator system, helping to detect exposure even when the toxic substance itself is impossible to measure.

One such test is the Clifford Materials Reactivity Test Clifford Consulting and Research, Box 17597, Colorado Springs, CO., 80935; ph. (719-550-0008). This test may be useful as a risk assessment tool to help the dentist or physician select appropriate dental materials, especially in the environmentally compromised or highly allergic patient. This is the only test of its kind that has received provisional approval of the International Academy of Oral Medicine and Toxicology.

PRECAUTIONS DURING REMOVAL

The removal of dental mercury fillings is accomplished by drilling. This procedure, by it's very nature, produces friction and heat which in turn causes some of the mercury in the fillings being removed to vaporize. Micro-particles of filling dust are also produced.[1-3] Consequently, there is always a risk of some mercury exposure during the filling removal procedure. This risk can be minimized with several precautions. Since the precautions are relatively simple, every patient should be protected. For the average healthy patient, only a few of these procedures may be necessary. While for the medically compromised individual, all the recommendations should be employed. Immediate acute side effects of mercury exposure that may result from the dental drilling procedure:

Headache
Nausea
Metals allergic reaction
Rash face/shoulders
Increased temperature

The condition is often described as flu-like.

The following are precautions that should be taken to limit mercury exposure during mercury filling removal.

1. Activated charcoal

Approximately 15-30 minutes before amalgam removal, one should take a charcoal caplet. This supplement will bind some of the minute amalgam particles that may be inadvertently swallowed during the drilling procedure. A second caplet should be taken at the end of the appointment. Thereafter, activated charcoal should be avoided because it can also absorb certain good nutrients in your vitamin program.

2. Room fans for ventilation

An excellent method to protect both the patient and the dentist is to have a small fan placed on the left of the patient (if the dentist is right handed) that will blow a stream of air across the patient towards their feet. Any vapors or particulate material are kept out of the breathing zone.

3. Eye protection

The eye is very sensitive and delicate and should be protected from exposure to mercury particles. Dental tooth surgery always produces an aerosol of vapor, fluid droplets and tooth and/or filling particles. It is just good practice to protect the patient's eyes with goggles when undertaking any tooth drilling. This protection will eliminate the possibility of physical damage to the eye that could result from trauma of filling material falling in the eye, and protect the sensitive eye from allergic or local toxic reactions. The dentist and his staff should also wear eye protection.

4. Protective coverings

The use of a large plastic drape over the patient is also recommended. This protects the patient from immediate exposure to filling particles on the skin and ensures that the clothes do not collect mercury-filling dust, which would be transported home. For the very sensitive patient, cloth drapes can be placed over the face.

5. Rubber dam

Rubber dam is a thin sheet of rubber that is placed in the mouth over the teeth with only the tops of the teeth protruding through.

Use of this rubber isolation procedure has several <u>advantages.</u>

a. A dry working field is maintained for the dentist because the rubber holds back the saliva.

b. The rubber dam protects the patient from possible inadvertent injury from the high-speed drill and ensures that foreign objects are not swallowed.

c. The dentist is also protected, since saliva and body fluids are held back, reducing the potential for infection.

d. The rubber dam does not allow the drilled particles of the removed mercury filling to be swallowed, nor does mercury vapor diffuse across the oral tissues into the bloodstream.

There are <u>no significant disadvantages</u> to using the rubber dam, except to those few individuals who may be allergic to the latex in the dam material. But, some circumstances are difficult, if not impossible, for rubber dam use. The rubber dam takes extra time, but it is the safest way to do dental treatment. Finally, some find the rubber dam uncomfortable or claustrophobic. These personal difficulties should be discussed thoroughly with your dentist.

6. Alternate source of breathing air

Since during removal of the filling some mercury vaporizes, an alternate source of breathing air is essential for the medically compromised or suspected mercury sensitive patient. Compressed medical air delivered to the patient through either a nose piece or nasal canula is the best method. This ensures that the risk to breathing the mercury vapor and dust is reduced. This protocol will significantly reduce the incidence of unwanted side effects as previously discussed.

7. A suction device CLEAN-UP™

This device, designed in Sweden and sold in North America, slips over the tooth to be treated and will suction away considerably more mercury vapor and particles than the standard dental suction devices. Highly recommended. Ask your dentist.

8. High pressure drills

Using the 90-psi drill, the dentist should section the mercury fillings. By sectioning the mercury filling, less drilling time is necessary and therefore less mercury vapor is produced.

9. High volume suction

Most dental offices are equipped with high volume suction. Sometimes, due to the large amount of water recommended, one vacuum tip is not sufficient. Some dentists will employ two such vacuums. The vacuum removes the water and particles, but also helps to reduce the mercury vapor and particle exposure.

10. Copious amounts of cool water

During the removal process, it is very important to spray copious amounts of <u>cool</u> water on the area where the drilling is occurring. The water must be cool and should be coming from the dental hand piece as well as independently from an air/water syringe. This serves several important functions. First, it cools the tooth, helping to prevent heat trauma to the delicate nerves and blood vessels in the pulp of the tooth. Second, it cools the mercury filling, greatly reducing the amount of mercury vaporization. Third, the water will minimize dust and particulate material from becoming airborne.

11. Method of filling removal

Most dental drills operate at approximately 30 pounds per square inch (psi.) This pressure is not sufficient to result in rapid filling removal. There are more appropriate dental drills that can operate up to 90 psi. When applied to the dental filling they cause the filling to fracture into large pieces. Thus, excessive drilling and grinding is avoided and mercury vapor release due to the removal process is kept to a minimum. This also limits the heat applied to the tooth and is therefore gentler to the nerve, reducing post-treatment tooth sensitivity.

LIFE-STYLE
MODIFICATIONS

In contrast to recognizable diseases that have scientifically established causes, chronic health problems are difficult to diagnose and treat, because of the non-specific nature of the symptoms and because of the variation of the symptoms from one individual to the next. Moreover, chronic poor health, as opposed to outright disease, is often a multi-factorial problem. Thus, poor nutrition, psychological distress, dental mercury exposure, environmental exposure to contaminants etc., when occurring in conjunction, may precipitate the poor health profile, especially in the genetically susceptible person. Consequently, you should attend to as many of these life style factors as possible to improve your overall health status.

THE SIMPLE DIET EXPERIMENT:
If possible and time permits prior to filling removal, one should do the "Simple Diet Experiment", <u>under the supervision of a physician or trained dentist.</u>

First, have your blood assessed for:
1. Total cholesterol (the good and bad cholesterol),

2. High density lipoproteins (the good cholesterol),

3. Low density lipoproteins (the bad cholesterol),

4. Triglycerides,

5. Blood sugar,

6. Uric acid,

7. Total protein,

8. Calcium and phosphorus

These are used to determine whether these indices of your body biochemistry fall within the "normal" range (normal may vary depending upon the philosophy of the practitioner and the laboratory used).

Immediately make the following dietary changes for 10-14 days and then have the blood profile repeated.
1. Eliminate all caffeine. (Coffee, tea, cola, chocolate etc.)

2. Eliminate all high sugar containing products.

3. Eliminate all red meat and organ meat (e.g. liver)

4. Eliminate all refined fats. (e.g. deep fried foods and butter)

5. Eliminate all milk and milk products (cheese etc), eggs and wheat products because these are known to have a high allergy incidence in the general population.

6. Eliminate all alcohol consumption.

7. Have at least one fresh salad a day with expeller pressed safflower oil or cold pressed virgin olive oil dressing.

8. Have at least two fresh fruits per day.

9. Increase the amount of fresh free-range poultry and small fish species eaten. (Do not eat swordfish, tuna, shark or other fish known to be high in mercury).

10. Drink at least eight glasses of room temperature water per day,

two being warm water with freshly squeezed lemon juice immediately in the a.m. on rising and just before bedtime.

11. Avoid nutritional (vitamin and mineral) supplementation.

12. Eat fresh foods rather than canned or processed foods that contain many additives.

Repeat your blood chemistry profile and note how you are feeling.

Dietary distress is a common problem in our culture and has been defined as "overconsumption/undernutrition".[1] In other words; we tend to eat empty foods devoid of nutrient value. These high-calorie refined foods supply energy but not the essential vitamins, minerals and essential amino and fatty acids necessary for proper maximum health. They are also very difficult to digest and often cause bloating.

Note: Today, some meat, including chicken and beef, are raised on ground fish meal. Many lake and large ocean-going fish are contaminated with organic methyl mercury. So, be cautious.

• ELIMINATE UNNECESSARY CHEWING:
Research discussed previously demonstrates that chewing is the main factor that causes mercury to be released from the mercury dental fillings. Therefore it is prudent to reduce your daily chewing times.

This can be accomplished by-.

1. Only having 2-3 meals per day.

2. Eliminate excessive snacking.

3. Eliminate chronic gum chewing.

4. Eliminate chewing foods that are thermally hot, salty or acidic, because they tend to enhance corrosion of the dental fillings and facilitate mercury release.

If you suffer from chronic tooth grinding behavior especially when you sleep, professional dental help should be sought. Wearing a mouth protective appliance will help eliminate the grinding and thus decrease the mercury vapor exposure that results from this grinding.

- **ELIMINATE OR REDUCE SMOKING.**

- **INCREASE YOUR EXERCISE.**

There are many excellent books on improving your health through exercise. Seek professional help especially if you are chronically ill or suffer serious medical disease.

- **AVOID PRODUCTS WITH TOXIC METALS.**
  Lead
  > Lead batteries
  > Auto exhaust
  > Lead water pipes
  > Fumes from unleaded gas (farms)
  > Cigarette smoke

  Aluminum
  > Pots and pans
  > Deodorants
  > Fruit, beer, drink cans

  Cadmium
  > Cigarette smoking
  > Some smelting industries

  Copper
  > Acid water in copper pipes
  > Soft drink dispensers
  > Copper cookware
  > Certain foods[2]
  >> Oysters
  >> Calf liver
  >> Instant Breakfast
  >> Tea bag
  >> Cocoa powder
  >> Duck liver
  >> Beef liver

Mercury
Coal burning
Mercury batteries
Large deep sea fish and fish from known polluted lakes.
Dental mercury fillings
Broken thermometers, Barometers etc.
Skin lightening creams
Laxatives containing Calomel
Some contact lens solutions
Water proof mascara

Contact with base metal costume jewelry

- **ELIMINATE CHRONIC INFECTIONS.**

Chronic infections such as fungal (yeast) are common in those with a history of birth control usage, chronic antibiotic usage, and immune related diseases. SEEK PROFESSIONAL MEDICAL DIAGNOSIS AND TREATMENT. Chronic mouth infections such as periodontal disease (gum infections) must be treated. These conditions can result from bacterial, fungal, viral, and amoebic parasites as well as medical conditions such as diabetes, blood disease and certain hormone dysfunctions. Impacted, dead and root canalled teeth should also be accessed.

10

CHEMICALLY SENSITIVE PATIENTS

"In the last quarter of the twentieth century, man suddenly finds himself living on an alien planet. He hasn't been there before, and his body doesn't know how to adapt. Since he first appeared on earth, he's gone through something like 175,000 generations - and all of them, until recently, ate generally the same kind of food, drank the same water, breathed the same air. Now all of this has changed. .... In only a sliver of evolutionary time, man has drastically transformed the world. ... Natural selection shaped our ancestors to make them superbly able to deal with their environment. Over the last half century or so, however, two things have happened to change that environment. First, the world has experienced a chemical avalanche. Second, man has polluted his air, his water, and his food. And now the environment is striking back in ways we have only begun to grasp. The human being is an accommodating animal, but evolution is slow, and the environmental changes are occurring much faster than man can adapt."[1]

Dr. Alfred Zamm

This quotation succinctly sums up the situation that Man finds himself in today. To these dramatic environmental changes Dr. Zamm could have added mercury exposure from dental fillings. Dental amalgam mercury is a double-edged sword. Not only does mercury act as a poison and an allergen, but it also destroys the very chemical processes that your body employs to detoxify itself.

The bulk of this chapter is a precis on the excellent text <u>Nutrition, Stress, and Toxic Chemicals: An Approach to Environmental-Health Controversies.</u> By Dr. AJ Vander. Toxic environmental chemicals fit into the following categories:[2]

1. <u>Excessive ingestion of nutrient chemicals.</u> Too much of a good thing can be harmful. For example, too much of the fat-soluble vitamins such as vitamin A will have toxic consequence. Also, daily consumption of selenium, when too high, becomes toxic.

2. <u>Exposure to naturally occurring bacterial, fungal and plant toxins.</u>

3. <u>Exposure to naturally occurring nonnutritive inorganic elements.</u> In this category are such elements as mercury, lead, cadmium, and arsenic.

4. <u>Synthetic chemicals.</u> Here are pesticides, food additives, herbicides, fertilizers etc.

These chemicals, which pervade our environment, are often derivatives of petrochemicals such as volatile organic hydrocarbons, aliphatic and aromatic hydrocarbons and pesticides.

XENOBIOTICS

Xenobiotics is the study of the effects of foreign chemicals upon living systems. The living systems have specialized tissues, organs and cells facilitating the elimination of these foreign substances. Within cells, biochemical pathways exist to inactivate foreign chemicals. These biochemical processes are commonly called the detoxification system. All chemicals, whether they are nutrients or toxins, must be altered biochemically so that the cell can either use or inactivate them and eventually excrete them.

47

UPTAKE OF XENOBIOTIC SUBSTANCES

Ingestion of a chemical does not necessarily mean it will reach the blood stream from the digestive tract. Many chemicals are unstable, affected by stomach acidity and bacteria or have chemical structures and size that do not absorb. These chemicals will pass through the digestive system with little or no effect. Other chemicals can cross the digestive tract membranes to the blood stream by diffusion or active transport. Diffusion is the natural movement of a substance from an area of high concentration to that of low concentration. Active transport, on the other hand, entails specialised receptor sites in the membrane and energy-dependent chemical mechanisms to trap the chemical and draw it across the membrane. The physical structure of the chemical is also important. Molecules can be lipid (fat) soluble (such as mercury) or lipid-insoluble. This characteristic depends on whether the molecule has an electrical charge. Those molecules that are nonpolar (without charge) tend to be lipid-soluble, while those that are polar (with a charge) are not. Lipid soluble compounds have little difficulty crossing the placenta to the developing foetus. The rise in birth defects (approximately 2% of the live births), the increasing incidence of spontaneous abortions (estimated to be approximately 20% of pregnancies) and the undocumented incidence of more subtle birth defects, all raise concern about xenobiotic exposures.[2] In this regard, mercury vapor is nonpolar and lipid soluble, and therefore, easily crosses lung cell membranes and oral mucosa membranes. But, mercury in the liquid metallic form is poorly absorbed across the intestinal tract. Methyl mercury, on the other hand, readily absorbs across intestine by active transport.

Metallic substances such as mercury, lead, and cadmium, must depend upon membrane carrier mediation (active transport) in the intestine to gain entrance into the blood stream. Thus, they compete with needed metallic nutrients (zinc, copper, calcium, etc.) upon which normal transport mechanisms depend. This competition not only allows some toxic metals to cross the membrane, but it reduces the essential trace element uptake. The effect is that tissues are exposed to the toxin and become depleted of the essential nutrient metals needed biochemically to aid in detoxification.[2] In contrast to the digestive tract, skin uptake of most toxic materials is by simple diffusion. This is true for mercury.

The respiratory tract consists of the nose, oral/nasal pharynx, the brachial tree and the lungs. Many gaseous chemicals (including mercury vapor from amalgam fillings) and fine particulate material can enter the body via this route. The tiny alveolar sacs (small air sacs in the lungs) will allow mercury vapor and small metallic particles an entrance into the body. Yet, the entire respiratory tract has many lines of defense.[2] First, the nose hairs and mucous membranes trap much of the foreign material. Second, the bronchial system is coated with mucous and hair-like projections called cilia that trap the foreign material and push it back out. Finally, at the air sacs are many specialized immune cells called macrophages. These scavenge the foreign material and digest it with strong enzymes, converting the toxic material to benign, excretable substances.

XENOBIOTIC TISSUE DISTRIBUTION

Once the toxin has gained entry to the blood, the first line of defense is the plasma proteins.[2] The binding of mercury, however, occurs more to the lipoproteins of the red blood cell wall. Within cells are intracellular proteins that act as storage depots.[2] A specific example is a protein called metal lothionein, specific for metals such as lead, cadmium and mercury and also for essential metals like zinc. A DNA-Mrna protein biochemical pathway controls the availability of this protein. When the blood and intracellular concentration of a toxic metal such as mercury rises, this induces the production of more intracellular metal lothionein. Thus, the toxin is bound up. Another common storage site for toxins is fat cells. This is especially true of fat-soluble chemicals that do not necessarily bind to the fat, but instead dissolve in it. Thus, if a person fasts or otherwise undergoes rapid weight loss, the toxins are released from the tissue into the blood. This can produce a sudden toxic shock to the person as some of the toxin redistributes to other tissues. Such circumstances place excessive stress on detoxifying organs like the liver and kidney.

As general rules:

a. Dieting for rapid weight loss should not accompany detoxification procedures. Avoid fasting.

b. Dietary and nutritional supplementation programs can be designed to help reduce the side effects of detoxification while encouraging elimination of the offending chemicals.

EXCRETION OF XENOBIOTIC CHEMICALS

There are three major routes of elimination: the respiratory tract, the gastrointestinal tract and the kidney. A fourth minor route of elimination is via the skin through sweating.

Loss via the respiratory tract is limited to gaseous chemicals, while the kidneys and gastrointestinal tract handle a wider variety of chemical forms. The kidneys will excrete substances that are soluble in the urine. The kidney filtering system is aided by diffusion and secretion, but counteracted to some extent by reabsorption, especially pronounced for lipid-soluble chemicals. Thus, the urine can contain chemicals at higher concentrations than found in blood. The gastrointestinal excretion results from the liver detoxifying chemicals and then excreting them via the bile. Again, this is counteracted by the re-absorption of biliary substances in the intestine.

General rules during detoxification that should be applied after removal of the mercury/silver fillings include:

1. Large quantities of water should be consumed daily (8-10 glasses) during detoxification to aid kidney elimination.

2. A high fiber diet during detoxification would be useful in decreasing the transit time of fecal material and thus not allowing time for biliary reabsorption in the intestine.

3. Activities that induce sweating will aid in toxin excretion (e.g. exercise, steam and saunas etc.)

DETOXIFICATION

The <u>first critical step</u> in helping the individual exposed chronically to mercury is the proper removal of the source of the exposure, which in most cases is the dental mercury fillings. The <u>second critical step</u> is to follow the previous lifestyle guidelines.

Large doses of vitamins and minerals, if taken as supplementation to your diet, are to be considered DRUGS. This implies that you be extremely cautious. Remember, vitamins, minerals and herbs can have serious side effects. In addition, they can interact with your regular medications, prescribed by your physician or dentist. A little may be good, but a lot can be harmful. Because of individual response variation to vitamin supplementation, it is inappropriate to recommend extensive therapy in a book of this nature. However, a basic program consistent with general health recommendations can be outlined. PROFESSIONAL SUPERVISION IS ALWAYS RECOMMENDED ESPECIALLY FOR THE SEVERELY MEDICALLY COMPROMISED PERSON.

YOU MUST BE ON THE SIMPLE DIET AS DESCRIBED PREVIOUSLY. To that diet you should add foods high in sulfur: for example, beans, onions, garlic and lentils. Eggs and lean red meat, also high in sulfur, should be used in moderation.

When possible prior to filling removal, commence the following vitamin regime. If you experience any untoward side effects, immediately cease supplementation and report to your medical/dental supervisor.

- **VITAMIN SUPPLEMENTATION**
1. <u>General B Complex Stress Formulation</u> 15-25 milligrams of each of the B vitamins): 1 tablet or capsule per day with breakfast.

2. <u>Vitamin C</u> (1000 milligrams time-release): 1 tablet with breakfast and I tablet with the evening meal.

3. <u>Zinc</u> (amino acid chelate 15-30 milligrams): 1 tablet after the evening meal.

4. <u>Selenium</u> (50-150 microgram): 1 tablet or capsule per day after lunch. Selenium can be found in a variety of foods such as: Butter, Brazil and cashew nuts, wheat germ and bran, brown rice, brewer's yeast, garlic and cheddar cheese.

5. <u>Vitamin E</u> (400 IU): 1 capsule per day taken after lunch.

6. <u>Vitamin A</u> (10,000 IU): 1 capsule per day.

7. <u>Acidophilus capsule:</u> 1 capsule before breakfast and 1 capsule prior to bedtime.

Some individuals are sensitive to yeast-based vitamin compounds or the binders that hold the tablets together. If you are such a person, most health food stores carry yeast-free products.

<u>If after your filling removal</u> you experience no problems, stay on the above protocol for 60 days. Do not stop vitamin therapy abruptly. Rather, slowly decrease the dosages of each vitamin by half weekly. If you wish, a general vitamin and mineral formulation can be taken as a daily supplement to your diet. DO NOT USE MEGADOSES WITHOUT PROFESSIONAL SUPERVISION.

<u>If after your filling removal</u> you experience negative effects:
1. Increase your vitamin C (1000 milligrams time-release) to 1 capsule three times per day for 30 days and then start reducing the dosages as described, especially if you experience diarrhea.

2. If the negative effects are intestinal (upset stomach, bloating, and gas) then add cultured dairy products to the diet (yogurt, cottage cheese, and buttermilk).

• SWEAT THERAPY

One of the primary modes of excretion of mercury is via the skin through sweat. Therefore, saunas or steam baths are excellent. If your health permits, perspiration producing exercise will not only tone you up and burn off excess calories, but the sweating will help eliminate mercury.

• OTHER THERAPIES.

Other therapies are available but necessitate MEDICAL supervision. Chelating drugs stimulate the release of mercury from body tissues. However, these medications may have side effects. Such drugs are BAL, EDTA, DMPS, DMSA, and D-Penicillamine (not to be confused with penicillin - antibiotic) Medical assessment and supervision is essential. Doctors familiar with these procedures are usually members of the American College of Advancement in Medicine (Suite 204; Laguna Hills, CA 92653 phone: 714-583-7666 on the World Wide Web at www.acam.org

Such medical intervention is not needed for everyone.

12

CONCLUSION:

"Prejudice means literally pre-judgement, the rejection of a contention out of hand, before examining the evidence. Prejudice is the result of powerful emotions, not of sound reasoning ... If after carefully and openly examining the evidence, we reject the proposition, that is not prejudice. It might be called "post-justice," It is certainly a prerequisite for knowledge."

Carl Sagan, Astrophysicist, Broca's Brain

The dental profession is in denial. Dentists cannot believe that their "experts" are wrong on the mercury filling question, despite scientific evidence to the contrary. Rationalizations such as the following are common:

"It is possible that the 'cures' are related to allergy. But do we ban the product because it has allergic potential? Patients die every year from penicillin. Do we ban it? Every drug has the potential to be toxic - every one! Do we ban all drugs."[1]

Of course, this fallacy is obvious. **Amalgam is not a drug.** It is a restorative dental material - AN IMPLANT, which by its very definition should do no harm. Attempts are also made to belittle the significance of the dental fillings as a source of toxic mercury. For example, many dental educators have go qualms about belittling the issue by suggesting that:

"Amalgam then becomes one of the numerous environmental issues that are an ever-increasing component of modem life. The ability to measure the mercury increase in bodily fluids and tissue with sensitive instrumentation does not make mercury a greater threat, it just calls attention to mercury" presence."

Dr. Irwin Mandel, Columbia University,

This is an incredible point of view, considering that in the almost 200 years of amalgam usage, the dental profession has not attempted to scientifically determine if mercury exposure from dental amalgams fillings is a health risk.

One should keep in mind Darwin's famous quote:

"False facts are highly injurious to the progress of science, for they often endure long; but false views, if supported by some evidence, do little harm, for everyone takes a salutary pleasure in proving their falseness; and when this is done, one path toward error is closed and the road to truth is often at the same time opened."

In this modern era of medicine, a substance is not deemed safe, unless it can be proven so with clear experimental research evidence!

American dental spokespersons give the same basic message, especially to the revelations of CBS NEWS 60 MINUTES on December 16, 1990. The key question that continues to surface as one examines this problem is "Where is the dental professions' legitimate scientific evidence, supporting their opinion of mercury filling safety?" What we continue to receive is mere rhetoric, not substance.

Dental mercury advocates, whose minds are prejudiced by their authoritarian dental education, by the propaganda of their professional associations, and by their own economic vested interests, claim (without scientific justification) that dental mercury fillings **must** be safe! In the absence of evidence they try to claim the high ground.

They claim that...

"The response [of the ADA] has been based on scientific evidence and ethical principle and has provided the opportunity to reaffirm and define dentistry's commitment to professionalism and ethical behavior."

Professionalism? Ethical behavior? Hardly!

As one might expect, the dental profession has not responded well to these data. Some national dental associations have attempted to influence public and governmental opinion by endorsing quasi-academic symposia pervaded with amalgam advocates. These gatherings are non-consensus meetings often under government auspices, where the moderators responsible for drawing the conclusions are typically inclined toward the prevailing dental orthodoxy and the conclusions reached often blatantly disregard the experimental data presented. Most damning to the dental profession is that they have not advanced any reputable experimental evidence of their own to support their belief in mercury filling safety.

The medical research evidence has been clear for some time. Dental amalgam - mercury fillings - constitutes a significant source of chronic exposure to mercury in the general population. This exposure is unnecessary and cannot be justified by risk/benefit analysis. While incriminating medical research continues to be published, the dental profession persists in placing itself in the untenable predicament of advocating an anecdotal position of mercury filling safety. The mercury filling advocates can be criticized for their shortage of supporting research evidence; however, so can many mercury filling opponents, who irresponsibly go far beyond the limits of the experimental data, by suggesting that miraculous cures will occur after removal of the fillings. Still, the mercury exposure from dental silver amalgam is toxicologically significant and research into its possible effects is at an early stage. Perhaps a 1000 years from now, historians will look back and draw comparisons between the chronic lead poisoning of the Roman Empire and the insidious mercury poisoning from our toxic teeth.

Use the information in this book to protect the health of your family and yourself because those controlling dentistry, caught in the vortex of a paradigm shift, appear to be unable or unwilling to protect your interests before their own!

13

EPILOGUE
- THE POLITICS

In 1987, the government of Sweden commissioned an "expert panel" to evaluate the available evidence regarding mercury filling safety. The panel concluded that mercury fillings were "unsuitable from a toxicological point of view". Based on this panel's advice, the Swedish Socialstyrelsen announced that steps would be taken to eliminate dental amalgam usage and recommended that comprehensive mercury filling treatment on pregnant women should be stopped to prevent mercury damage to the fetus.[1] Shortly thereafter, the German Ministry of Health (Bundesgesundheitsamt, BDA) issued a similar advisory.[2] In October of 1989, the Swedish Director of Chemical Inspection (KEMI), responsible for environmental protection, declared that amalgam would be banned.[3] In January of 1992, the German Ministry of Health (BDA) informed manufacturers of its intention to ban the production of amalgam.[4] The BDA removed low copper non-gamma-2-amalgam from the market and published a pamphlet recommending avoiding mercury filling use in individuals with kidney disease, children to age 6, and pregnant women.[5] In August of 1992, the Swedish government suggested a timetable to phase out mercury fillings. Environmental concerns were used as the official reason for amalgam discontinuation, but the government did acknowledge the toxicological risk to patients and stated that mercury fillings should no longer be used in children by July 1993, in adolescents to age 19 by July 1995, and in all Swedish citizens by 1997.[6] The Austrian Minister of Health announced that the use of mercury fillings in children would be banned in 1996 and discontinued in all Austrians by the year 2000.[7] In 1994, the Swedish Dental Association acknowledged that its leadership had previously been incorrect in their position regarding mercury filling safety. They now support a discontinuation of mercury use in dentistry.[8] Other industrialized countries, for what ever reason, appear to be side stepping the issue.

It should come as no surprise to find that recently, Health Canada has come out in support of the scientific research. Even after much political pressure from organized dentistry, the following recommendations were published on August 21, 1996 and sent to every dentist and physician in Canada.

HEALTH CANADA POSITION STATEMENT ON DENTAL AMALGAM

Considerations:
1. Although dental amalgam is the single largest source of mercury exposure for average Canadians, current evidence does not indicate that dental amalgam is causing illness in the general population. However, there is a small percentage of the population, which is hypersensitive to mercury and can suffer severe health effects from even a low exposure.

2. A total ban on amalgam is not considered justified. Neither is the removal of sound amalgam fillings in patients who have no indication of adverse health effects attributable to mercury exposure.

3. As a general principle, it is advisable to reduce human exposure to heavy metals in our environment, even if there is

no clinical evidence of <u>adverse health effects, provided</u> the reduction can be achieved at reasonable cost and <u>without introducing other adverse effects.</u>

Recommendations:

Health Canada advises dentists to take the following measures:

1. Non-mercury filling materials should be considered for restoring the primary teeth of children where the mechanical properties of the material are suitable.

2. Whenever possible, amalgam fillings should not be placed in or removed from the teeth of pregnant women.

3. Amalgam should not be placed in patients with impaired kidney function.

4. In placing and removing amalgam fillings, dentists should use techniques and equipment to minimize the exposure of the patient and the dentist to mercury vapor, and to prevent amalgam waste from being flushed into municipal sewage systems.

5. Dentists should advise individuals who may have allergic hypersensitivity to mercury to avoid the use of amalgam. In patients, who have developed hypersensitivity to amalgam, existing amalgam restorations should be replaced with another material where this is recommended by a physician.

6. New amalgam fillings should not be placed in contact with existing metal devices in the mouth, such as braces.

7. Dentists should provide their patients with sufficient information to make an informed choice regarding the material used to fill their teeth, including information on the risks and benefits of the material and suitable alternatives.

8. Dentists should acknowledge the patient's right to decline treatment with any dental material.

<u>A word of caution:</u> At first glance, it would appear that science has won out. However, Health Canada has left it up to the Provincial Dental Associations to monitor and enforce the recommendations. Need more be said!

BIBLIOGRAPHY

Introduction

1. Doherty, H.F.: Fighting for Organised Dentistry: An Interview with Incoming ADA president Geraldine T. Morrow, Dentistry Today p 32, September 1991

Chapter 1

1. Phillips, R.W. (1982): <u>Skinner's science of dental materials</u>, 8th ed. Philadelphia: W.B. Saunders Co, 311.

2. Paterson, N. (1984): The longevity of restorations. Br Dent J 157:23-5.

3. Phillips, R.W.; Hamilton, A.I.; Jendresen, M.D.; McHorris, W.H.;and Schallhorn, R.G. (1986): Report of Committee on Scientific Investigation of the American Academy of Restorative Dentistry. J Prosth Dent 55:736-72.

4. Bauer, J.G. and First, H.A. (1982): The toxicity of mercury in dental amalgam, Calif. Dent. J., 10:47-61.

Chapter 2

1. American Academy of Dental Science, <u>A history of dental and oral science in. America.</u> Philadelphia: Samuel White, publ., 1876

2. Bremmer, D.K., <u>The story of dentistry,</u> revised 3rd ed. Brooklyn: Dental Items of Interest Publishing Co Inc., 1954

3. Ring, M., <u>Dentistry an illustrated history,</u> Harryu N. Abrams Inc., Publisher, New York, 1985.

4. Stock, A., *Z Angew Chemie,* 1926, 39, 984-989.

5. Stock, A., *Z Angew Chemie,* 1928, 41, 663-72.

6. Stock, A., *Z Anorg Allgem Chemie,* 1934, 217, 241-53.

7. Stock, A., *Naturwissch,* 1935, 28, 453-6.

8. Stock, A., *Arch Gewerbepath Gewerbehygie,* 1936, 388-413.

9. Stock, A., *Ber Dtsch Chem Ges,* 1939,72,1844-57.

10. American Dental Association, Principle of ethics and code of professional conduct., section I-J; Representation of care and fees, 211 E. Chicago Avenue, Chicago IL U.S.A., 60611.

11. When your Patient asks about mercury in amalgam, J Amer Dent Assn, 120:39611990.

12. ADA letter, 22 May 1986. John W. Stanford, Phd., Secretary, ADA Council on Dental Materials, Equipment and Devices.

13. Final Rule. Dental Devices: General provisions and classification 110 devices. Federal Register 52(155):30082-106, 12 Aug 1987.

14. Recommendations in Dental Mercury Hygiene, ADA Council on Dental Materials, Instruments and Equipment. J Amer Dent Assn 109:617-19, 1984.

Chapter 3

1 . ADA (1984): To the Dental Patient, ADA News, Jan. 2

2. Vimy, M.J. and Lorscheider, F.L. (1985): Intra-oral air mercury released from dental amalgam. J Dent Res 64:1069-71.

3. Vimy, M.J. and Lorscheider, F.L. (1985): Serial measurements of intra-oral air mercury: Estimation of daily dose from dental amalgam. J Dent Res 64:1072-5.

4. Patterson, J.E.; Weissberg, B.G.; and Dennison, P.J. (1985): Mercury in human breath from dental amalgam. Bull Environ Contam Toxicol 34:459-68.

5. Fredin, B. (1988): Studies on the mercury release from dental amalgam fillings. Swed Dent J 3:8-15.

6. Schiele, R., Shellman, B., Schrodl, R. and Schaller, K.H. (1984) Untersuchungen zurn quicksilbergehalt von gehirn und nierin in abhangigkeit von zahl und zustand der amalgamfullungen. Inst fur arbeits und sozial-medizin, Universitat Erlanger-Nurenberg, Symp Forsch Inst Zahnarztl Versorg, Koln, West Germany, March.

7. Nylander, M., Friberg, L., and Lind, B. (1987): Mercury concentrations in the human brain and kidneys in relation to exposure from dental amalgam fillings. Swed. Dent. J. 11, 179-187.

8. Eggelston, D.W. and Nylander, M. (1987): Correlation of dental amalgam with mercury in brain tissue. J Prosth Dent 58:704-707.

9. Hahn, U., KJoiber, R., Leininger, R.W., Vimy, M.J. and Lorscheider, F.L. "Whole-body imaging of the distribution of mercury released from dental fillings into monkey tissues". FASEB J. 4: 3256-3260,1990.

10. WHO Task Group (1991): IPCS, Environmental Health Criteria 118: Inorganic Mercury World Health Organisation, Geneva.

11. Skare, I and Engquist, A. (1994): Human exposure to mercury and silver released from dental amalgam restorations. Arch Eviron Hlth, 949:384-94

12. Truono, E.J. (1991): Letter of Importance JADA 122:8-14.

13. ADA News Release (1990): ADA Reaffirms Safety & Effectiveness of Dental Amalgam.

14. Vimy, M.J., Takahashi, Y., and Lorscheider, F.L. (1990): Maternal-fetal distribuion of mercury (203-Hg) released from dental amalgam fillings. Am. J. Physiol. 258, R939-R945.

15. Boyd, N.D., Benediktsson, H., Vimy, M.J., Hooper, D.E. and Lorscheider, F. L. "Mercury from dental 'silver' tooth fillings impairs sheep kidney function". Amer. J. Physiol. 261: R1010-R1014,1991.

16. Thompson, C.M., Markesbery, W.R., Ehmann, W.D., Mao, Y-X. AND Vance D.E. Regional brain trace-element studies in Alzheimer's disease. Neurotoxicol 1988; 9, 1 -7.

17. Wenstrup, D., Ehmann, W.D. and Markesbery W.R. Trace element imbalances in isolated subcellular fractions of Alzheimer's disease brains. *Brain Res* 1990; 633, 125-131.

18. Duhr, E., Pendergrass, C., Kasarskis, E., Slevin, J. and Haley, B. Hg^{2+} induces GTP-tubulin interactions in rat brain similar to those observed in Alzheimer's disease. *FASES J* 1991; 6, A456.

19. Khatoon, S., Campbell, S.R., Haley, B.E. and Slevin, J.T. Aberrant guanosine triphosphate-beta-tubulin interaction in Alzheimer's disease. *Ann Neurol* 1989; 26, 210-215.

20. Pendergrass, J.C., Haley, B.E., Vimy, M.J., Winfield, S.A., and Lorscheider, F.L. "Mercury vapor inhalation inhibits binding of GTP to tubulin in rat brain: similarity to a molecular lesion in Alzheimer diseased brain." NeuroToxicology.18:315-324, 1997.

21. Vimy, M.J., Hooper, D.E., King, W.W., and Lorscheider, F.L. "Mercury from maternal 'silver' tooth fillings in sheep and human breast milk: A source of neonatal exposure." Biol. Trace Element Res., 56:143-152, 1997.

22. Summers, A.O., Wireman, J., Vimy, M.J., Lorscheider, F.L., Marshall, B., Levy, S.B., Bennett, S., and Billard, L. Mercury released from dental "silver" fillings provokes an increase in mercury and antibiotic resistant bacteria in primate oral and intestinal flora. Antimicrobial Agents & Chemotherapy, 37:825-834,1993.

23. Lorscheider, F.L., Vimy, M.J. and Summers, A.O. "Mercury exposure from "silver" tooth fillings: Emerging evidence questions a traditional dental paradigm." FASEB J. 9, 504-508,1995.

Chapter 4

1   Oettingen W.F. Poisioning a Guide to Clinical Diagnosis and Treatment, W.B. Saunders Co., Philadelphia, 1959.

2. Environmental Health Criteria I, Mercury. World Health Organization, Geneva, 1976.

3. Zifff S, and Ziff, M. 1988. The Hazards of Silver/Mercury Dental Fillings. Bio-probe Inc Orlando Fl.

Chapter 5

1 . Klaassen, C.D. 1985. Heavy metals and heavy metal antagonists. In: Gilman A, Goodman L, Rail T, Murad F, eds. Goodman and Gilman's pharmacological basis of therapeutics, 7th ed. New York: MacMillan Publ Co, 1611-14.

2. Bauer, J.G. and First, H.A. 1982. The toxicity of mercury in dental amalgam. Calif Dent Assoc J 10:47-61.

3. Rupp, N,W, and Paffenbarger, G.O. 1971, Significance to health of mercury used in dentistry: A review. J Am Dent Assoc 82:1401-7.

4. Markow, H. 1943. Urticaria following a dental silver filling - case report. NY State J Med 43:1648-52.

5. Djerassi, E. and Berova, N. 1969. The possibilities of allergic reactions from silver amalgam restorations. Int Dent J 19:481-8.

6. Bauer, J.G. and First, H.A. 1982. The toxicity of mercury in dental amalgam. Calif Dent Assoc J 10:47-61.

7. Mitchell, E.D.; Stanford, J.W.; Rupp, N.W.; Moffa, J.P.; Autian, J.; Fairhurst, C.W.; Millar, J.; and Reese, J. (1984): NIDR/ADA workshop on the biocompatibility of metals in dentistry. NIDR Bethesda, MD

8. North American Contact Dermatitis Group. Epidemiology of contact dermatitis in North America: 1972. Arch. Dermatol. 108:537-40, 1973.

9. Druet, P.; Hirsch, F.; Sapin, C.; Druet, E.; and Bellon, B. 1982. Immune dysregulation and autoimmunity induced by toxic agents. Transplant Proc 14:482-4.

10. Druet, P.; Hirsch, F.; Sapin, C.; Druet, E.; and Bellon, B. 1982. Immune dysregulation and autoimmunity induced by toxic agents. Transplant Proc 14:482-4.

11. Druet, P.; Bernard, A.; Hirsch, F.; Weening, J.J.; Gengoux, P.; Mahieu, P.; and Berkeland, S. 1982. Immunologically mediated glomerularnephritis induced by heavy metals. Arch Toxicol 50:187-94.

12. Stokinger, H.E. 1967. Testing for hypersusceptibility. Washington: Occupational Safety and Health Association, Natl Safety News 95(5):40.

13. Stokinger, H.E. 1970. Criteria and procedures for assessing the toxic responses to industrial chemicals. Permissible levels of toxic substances in the working environment. Geneva: International Labor Office, Occupational Safety and Health Series No. 20 36-52.

Chapter 6

1. Svare, C.W.; Peterson, L.C.; Reinhardt, J.W.; Boyer, D.B.; Frank, C.W.; Gay, D.D.; and Cox, R.D. 1981. The effects of dental amalgam on mercury levels in expired air. J Dent Res 60:1668-71.

2. Vimy, M.J. and Lorscheider, F.L. 1985. Intra-oral air mercury released from dental amalgam. J Dent Res 64:1069-71.

3. Vimy, M.J. and Lorscheider, F.L. 1985. Serial measurements of intra-oral air mercury: Estimation of daily dose from dental amalgam. J Dent Res 64:1072-5.

4. Aronsson, A.M., Lind, B,, Nylander, M. and Nordberg, M. (1989): Dental Amalgam and Mercury. Biol Metals 2:25-30.

5. Vimy, M.J. and Lorscheider, FL, Dental amalgam mercury daily dose estimated from intra-oral vapor measurements: A predictor of mercury accumulation in human tissues. J Trace Elem Exper Med 3:111-113, 1990.

6. Aposian et. al., (1992): Urinary mercury after administration of DMPS: correlation with dental amalgam score., FASEB J. 6:2472-2476.

7. Mackert, J.R. 1986. Correspondence reply. J Am Acad Dermatol 14:277-8.

Chapter 7

1 Hampton, E.L. (1980): Hampton's Textbook of Operative Dentistry. 4th ed. William Heinemannn Medical Books Ltd, London.

2. Phillips, R.W. (1982): Skinner's science of dental materials, 8th ed. Philadelphia: W.B. Saunders Co.

Chapter 8

1. Richards, J.M. and Warren, P.J. 1985. Mercury vapor released during the removal of old amalgam restorations. Br Dent J 159:231-2.

2. Wright, F. 1971. Allergic reaction to mercury after dental treatment. New Zealand Dent J 67:251-2.

3. Phillips, R.W. (1982): Skinner's science of dental materials, 8th ed. Philadelphia: W.B. Saunders Co, 311.

Chapter 9

1. Bland, J. ed. 1983. Medical Applications of Clinical Nutrition. Keats Publishing, New Canaan Connecticut, p. 5.

2. Pennington, J.T. and Calloway, D.H. 1973. Copper content of foods. Research 63:143-153.

Chapter 11

1. Zamm, A.V. (1980): Why Your House May Endanger Your Health. A Touchstone Book, Simon and Schuster, New York. Pp. 13-14.

2. Vander, A.J. (1981): Nutrition, Stress, and Toxic Chemicals: An Approach jo Environmental-Health Controversies. The University of Michigan Press, Ann Arbor, chpt 8 pp. 255-299.

Chapter 12

1. Katz, H.S. (1991): Unwarranted and unprofessional: the superfluous removal of clinically acceptable amalgams. Oper. Dent. 16:113-115.

2. Mandel, I.D. (1991): Living with amalgam: an environmental perspective, Quint. Int. 22:337-339.

3. Jones, D. Giving Science a Bad Name. J Can Dent 57:291-93.

4. Meshkin, L.H. (Ed. JADA), Views: "...Potential Unreasonable Risk..." ADA 122:8,1991.

5. Odom, J.G. (1991): Ethics and dental amalgam removal, JADA 122:69-71

Chapter 13

1. Socialstyrelsen (Sweden, Social Welfare and Health Administration). Redovisar; kvicksilver/amalgam halsorisker. Allanna Forlaget AB, Stockholm, 10 32-39,1987.

2. Bundesgesundheitsamt (Germany, Ministry of Health), Machine Design, p. 274, August 25,1988.

3. KEMI (Sweden, Chemical Inspection Agency), Amalgam will be banned. Dagens Nyheter, October 6, 1989.

4. Bundesgesundheitsamt (Germany, Ministry of Health), Letter to pharmacetical companies, January 29; Artezeitung (Physician's Daily), March 3, 1992

5. Bundesgesundheitsamt (Germany, Ministry of Health), Amalgame-nevbenwirkungen und bewertung der toxizitat, Zahnartzt Woche (DZW), 1992, 8, 1.

6. Socialstyrelsen (Sweden, Social Welfare and Health Administration), Press Release. August 28, 1992.

7. Austrian Minister of Health, Austria to be amalgam free by year 2000. FDI Dental World, March/April, 1993, p. 6.

8. Swedish Dental Association, Swedish News Bureau, TT January 17, 1994.

9. Lorscheider, F. L. and Vimy, M.J., FASEB J., 1993, 7, 1432-1433.